...aring

d's

et

sharing God's planet

a Christian vision for a sustainable future

a report from the Mission and Public Affairs Council

CHURCH HOUSE
PUBLISHING

Church House Publishing
Church House
Great Smith Street
London
SW1P 3NZ

Tel: 020 7898 1451
Fax: 020 7898 1449

ISBN 0 7151 4068 X

GS 1558

Published 2005 by Church House Publishing

Copyright © The Archbishops' Council 2005

This report has only the authority of the Council that approved it.

Cover design by Church House Publishing

Printed by Creative Print and Design Group Ltd, Ebbw Vale

contents

Sharing God's Planet was commissioned by the Church of England's Mission and Public Affairs Council and is commended by the Council as a contribution to study, discussion and action. It was written by Claire Foster, Policy Adviser for Science, Technology, Medicine and Environment for the Archbishops' Council.

foreword

Early modern religion contributed to the idea that the fate of nature is for it to be bossed around by a detached sovereign will, whether divine or human. As a counterbalance to this attitude of lofty separation, I want to suggest a Christian reason for regarding ecology as a matter of justice for the human and the non-human world.

Creation is an act of communication. It is God expressing his intelligence through every existing thing. The divine *logos* spoken of at the beginning of St John's Gospel is that by which everything comes to be. As Maximus the Confessor says, each existent reality is itself a *logos* – a word, an intelligible structure – which carries in its own specific, unique way the universal *logos* within it. This implies that each thing communicates the character of God, by virtue of the eternal Word.

So to penetrate the workings of the world, to understand its intelligible shape, is to come into contact with a divine action that is reasonable, consistent with itself. To understand, or more accurately to *hear*, that which the world communicates, is to *hear* God's love and God's glory. To do this, human beings have to tune in; quite simply, to listen, rather than to impose our own prejudiced interpretations of what the world ought to be. In the language of Jewish scripture, true thinking, true knowing of the world is becoming aligned with God's wisdom, which is God's self-consistency in purpose and action. This can be experienced and understood as a living principle in the universe *as it is*.

The Christian reason for regarding ecology as a matter of justice, then, is that God's self-sharing love is what animates every object and structure and situation in the world. Responses to the world that are unaware of this are neither truthful nor sustainable. To be aware of this is to enter into relationship, for the self-sharing love of God is not simply something we admire, but something in which we fully participate. We are not consumers of what God has made; we are in communion with it.

There is material in this volume that should help to effect a *metanoia*, a change of perception, that allows us to hear what the world is communicating, and to respond appropriately.

The vision of *contraction and convergence* as a response to climate change, which is described in this volume, is one that I support.
I have also called upon our Church to undertake an ecological audit of some sort; information about how to do this can be found in Part Three. Such local, internal responses are vital if our voice as a Church is to have integrity.

To these sophisticated responses to the ecological crisis I should like to add a call for simple, accessible ways of learning again what it is to be part of the created order. Receive the world that God has given. Go for a walk. Get wet. Dig the earth.

I commend this volume as a contribution to the Church's thinking on ecological justice.

✠ Rowan Cantuar

introduction

The earth is ailing, and every creature in it, including humankind, is affected. The evidence suggests that human activity, particularly in the last 100 years, has contributed significantly to the suffering. Humans treat the earth according to their perceptions of it. If people see each other as alien and the earth as inert matter, their behaviour will reflect that perception. If people see each other as part of the same family, and the earth as connected to them because of its sacred origin in the same God who made them, they may be motivated to live in harmony under God.

Nothing stands still, and earthly environmental change is as old as the planet itself. Change is not necessarily bad. It happens, and all that happens is within the gaze of the creator. A global perspective that puts God, not human beings, at the centre of everything would not necessarily assume that floods or hurricanes are bad events in and of themselves. They become bad in people's minds because of the consequent loss of human life and livelihood that can be counted and should be mourned. There may once have been floods in the place that is now called Bangladesh when there were no people living there, floods which, from the point of view of the overall balance of the earth's environment, were positively good.

Humanity is part of the environment too, however, and it would be as much of a mistake to ignore human claims to existence and thriving as it would for humans to ruin the environment for selfish gain. Both matter, because both come from the same divine source and exist by virtue of the one God's gracious love. The earth is ailing because anthropology and ecology are not treated holistically, and both are suffering the consequences.

The unitary, sacred origin of all that is informs the premise of this book, which is that it is possible and desirable for people to live and work within their environments, not as enemies, nor even as uneasy bedfellows, but harmoniously under God. If humanity can understand that all creatures, including humans, are under God, it might then use its God-given intelligence to find out how to 'safeguard the integrity of creation and sustain and renew the life of the earth' (the fifth mark of mission of the Anglican Communion) rather than thinking of the earth as an adversary and using human intelligence to dominate and control it.

The idea of nature as alien and frightening, needing to be commanded and controlled, has governed many human actions in the past and people still live under that legacy. This book will describe the size and magnificence of the world, and how well humans can live in it if they so choose. The book will also speak of human failure to live well, something for which, historically, Christians have been partly to blame because of the way they have interpreted their tradition. Within Christian teaching, however, there are insights that can undo some of the damage of the past.

outline of the book

The first part of the book will look at the history of Western human engagement with the environment, showing how thought patterns have contributed to human industrial and post-industrial treatment of the world. The focus is on Western thought because the readership of this book will largely consist of those living under its legacy. Part One will then investigate the ways in which humans may have caused harm in the different *spheres*: the *atmosphere* with pollution and overheating; the *hydrosphere* with water pollution and 'replumbing'; the *lithosphere* with mineral extraction; the *pedosphere* with soil erosion; and the *biosphere* with the expansion to 'rogue' status of the human species, the loss of other species' habitats and the threat to biological diversity on which every living thing depends. By describing the world in this way, as well as gaining an understanding of the effects of human activity, the reader should see the size and complexity of the world and the extraordinary intelligence of its Maker.

The second part of the book will begin to construct theological and biblical foundations for a loving, Christian perception of the world. These foundations will start with the basic teaching that the world was made by God and belongs to him, and human beings are stewards of the creation under God's sovereignty. Four theological principles will be explored to expand this role: God's covenant with creation; the sacrament of creation; the prophetic, priestly and kingly role of humanity; and the feast of the Sabbath. Fianlly, there are some topics for group discussion, a meditation, and some practical exercises to help the reader connect with the elements of the world.

The third part of the book will describe ways in which readers can start to live according to new perceptions that, it is hoped, will have been produced by reading thus far. This part includes suggestions for practical, community and spiritual activities for individuals and churches.

Part Four has a description of the main Christian environmental organizations and how to contact the Church of England Diocesan Environmental Officers, together with a list of useful web sites. This part ends with the references for this book, as well as other books that may be of interest for further reading.

part one

human impact
on the environment

introduction

It has to be recognized that, to an extent far beyond any other species, humanity is capable of, and indeed can hardly stop itself from, consciously transforming its environment. One way of understanding this is to see that, for the most part, animals and plants adapt to the environment in which they find themselves, whereas most humans attempt to make environments adapt to them. Human perception of the world and its place in it has informed the way it has gone about this adaptation, and Christianity has contributed to the way these perceptions and consequent attitudes have developed.

background

In the sixteenth and seventeenth centuries, scientific discoveries were predicated on the belief that the world was objectively observable and behaved mechanistically. Humans could harness the natural forces of the earth and make it serve them. They saw and experienced the earth as a storehouse of rich resources to which they could help themselves, so their engagement with the world was extractive, industrial and non-renewable. Christians will acknowledge that although the image of humankind having 'dominion' over the earth is a biblical one, it can become distorted into a justification for abuse and exploitation of the earth God has created. Thus, for example, the confident engineers of the Victorian era saw themselves as exercising their God-given right to command and control the world around them. Chicago businessman W. P. Rend said in 1892:

> Smoke is the incense burning on the altars of industry. It is beautiful to me. It shows that men are changing the merely potential forces of nature into articles of comfort for humanity.[1]

1

Darwin, Einstein and quantum mechanics

Darwinism and Einstein's theory of relativity[2] were counterweights to a human-centred view of the universe. Darwin's theory of evolution placed humanity in among the rest of creation, evolving along with it, and differing from other species only in degree. The theories of relativity and quantum mechanics indicated that the observer and the observed form an unbreakable unity, that different observers see differently from each other and that the universe in its remotest parts is present in every other single part of it. The belief that a human being was a detached observer, unaffected by his or her environment, was shown to be mistaken.

Christians need to face the consequences of a distorted understanding of humanity's place in the world that an overemphasis on human superiority and a neglect of corresponding human responsibility have produced. The theories of evolution and relativity should challenge a Christian to re-examine what the Bible actually teaches about humanity's place in the universe God created.

the twentieth century

The twentieth century saw a rise in secularism in the West, which supported the project of growth without limit. The need to develop materially became paramount, as happiness was seen as being something to enjoy now, on this earth, and not beyond it.

The freedom to use and abuse the earth could be contained while there was not too much of it going on. But there has never before been anything like the level of human intervention seen during the twentieth century,[3] and there is now great cause for concern. The extent to which humans altered their environments in order to live the lives they wanted was unprecedented. The level (rather than the intrinsic nature) of alteration of and interference with the earth upon which humanity is engaged is such that the earth may be reaching breaking point. These are the signs of the times to which environmental scientists and others are pointing, and the pictures of the future that they paint are not happy ones for the human species, nor for life on earth generally.

spheres of intervention

In the paragraphs that follow the level of human activity during the twentieth century will be explained in the context of the longer and larger story of the astonishing cosmos God has created. The descriptions will suggest that the experiments of technological intervention that have been engaged upon are uncontrolled, and the cumulative effect of increased activity and increased intensity of activity may be triggering irreversible and catastrophic step changes in the environment of the earth.

Human intervention in the environment can be seen in each of the *spheres* of the earth. These are: the *atmosphere*: the air and lower elevations of space; the *hydrosphere*: the salt waters and freshwaters that cover most of the earth and percolate far below it; the *lithosphere* and *pedosphere*: the rocks and soils that make up the land surface; and the biosphere: the community of all living things.

the atmosphere

The atmosphere is the thin gaseous envelope that surrounds the earth. It is about 100 km thick, although the outer boundary is arbitrary as it shades off gradually into outer space. Air contains thousands of gases, but two predominate: nitrogen (78 per cent) and oxygen (21 per cent). In the long term the chemistry of the atmosphere has changed, for example in the very early days of the earth many low-density gases were lost to outer space, and before there were plants on the earth there was not much oxygen. Now there are many cycles of motion of gases, created by changes of temperature in the outer regions of the atmosphere known as the stratosphere, and at the lowest altitudes by exchanges of heat, moisture and gases with soil, water and living things. The outermost regions of the atmosphere receive and reflect the all-important sun's rays.[4]

The gases in the atmosphere maintain a balance between them to make life possible. If such a balance were not maintained the planet could be more like Mars, whose average temperature is −23°C, or it could resemble Venus, where temperatures are above the boiling point of water. Not much needs to be done to the gases to alter conditions on earth fundamentally. The main gases in the atmosphere that have been affected by human activity are: carbon dioxide, ozone, sulphur dioxide, methane, chlorofluorocarbons (CFCs) and two nitrogen oxides. These can be divided into two groups: greenhouse gases that are of global significance; and other gases that are of regional significance.

greenhouse gases

The gases that are of global significance, because they remain in the atmosphere for a century or more and disperse around the world, are carbon dioxide, methane, CFCs and nitrous oxide. All these gases are called greenhouse gases because they trap the rays of the sun, which are essential for life, but which also heat the earth and potentially overheat the earth. Human sources of **carbon dioxide** are fossil fuel burning and deforestation. In 1990, 100 per cent of all emissions of carbon dioxide were from human activity. Between 1900 and 1990 the concentration of carbon dioxide in the atmosphere rose from 290,000 parts per billion by volume (ppbv) to 360,000 ppbv.

The human sources of **methane** are rice fields, livestock, waste, fossil fuel burning and mining. Its concentration in the atmosphere rose from 900 ppbv to 1,700 ppbv between 1900 and 1990. **CFCs**, produced only by human use of refrigerants, foams and aerosol sprays, as well as being greenhouse gases destroy ozone, itself a greenhouse gas present in small quantities in the stratosphere. From there being no CFCs in the atmosphere in 1900 there are now somewhere between 1 and 3 ppbv, which may not sound like much but is enough significantly to damage the ozone layer. The human causes of **nitrous oxide** are fertilizers, burning of organic matter and deforestation. Nitrous oxide causes acid rain and smog. Its levels rose during the twentieth century from 285 ppbv to 310 ppbv.

regional gases

Gases that are of regional significance, because they remain in the atmosphere only briefly and therefore do not disperse around the globe, are sulphur dioxide, nitrogen oxides and ozone. These are not greenhouse gases but have significant adverse effects on the atmosphere. **Sulphur dioxide** is produced by fossil fuel burning and ore smelting, and causes acid rain. Its quantity in 1900 was unknown; now it is something over 0.3 ppbv. **Nitrogen oxides**, from fossil fuel and biomass burning, cause acid rain and smog, and have risen to something over 0.001 ppbv during the twentieth century. Finally, **ozone**, measured only in western Europe's troposphere (the troposphere is 6–10 km above the ground) is produced by vehicle exhaust's interaction with sunshine, and causes smog. In the twentieth century it has risen from 10 ppbv to 20–40 ppbv. These rises in concentration of gases may or may not be significant. They are a largely uncontrolled experiment in altering the atmosphere that protects life on earth.

air pollution

In addition to gases, the atmosphere has been affected by the thousands of tons of potentially toxic metals that have been released into the air as dust, from fossil fuel burning, metal smelting and waste incineration. Some of this toxic dust has worked its way into the food chain to the detriment of, *inter alia*, fish, otters, alligators, mink, raccoons and eagles. Human health has suffered from lead emissions, mainly from cars. Urban air pollution dates from earlier times but in the twentieth century reached levels sufficient to kill, it is suggested, somewhere between 25 and 40 million people through respiratory disease.[5]

From 1950, more and more people came to live in cities like Mexico City and Calcutta, where air pollution remains a significant killer. In 1988 the World Health Organization estimated that of 1.8 billion city dwellers in the world, more than a billion breathed air with unhealthy levels of sulphur dioxide and soot or dust.[6]

reversals in damage to the atmosphere

Cities like London, and dozens of others in western Europe, North America and Japan, managed to bring air pollution under control through greater environmental awareness, regulation and new technologies. One simple test of the vast improvement in urban air pollution in these cities is that silver does not tarnish as it once did. However, the vast majority of the world's population are not yet enjoying such improved conditions.

In the international agreements on acid rain and ozone after 1975, ministers, heads of state and major corporations took part. The Montreal Protocol of 1987 and amendments has ensured that no more CFCs are being released into the atmosphere, but it will be at least a century before any change to the concentration is seen, because the residence time of CFCs is so long. For the most part, however, it has been found that when the cause of air pollution is dealt with, the consequences are reversible within a short space of time.

global warming

The warming of the atmosphere, however, has not been controlled. The acceleration of carbon dioxide emissions into the atmosphere from 1800 onwards, together with other greenhouse gases following industrialization, meant that heat from the sun was more effectively trapped. Soot and dust injected into the atmosphere slightly lowered the amount of solar energy reaching the earth's surface. The slight increase in the warmth of the earth during the twentieth century was probably due to these factors.

The consequences of this slight warming were relatively small, with some changing of habitats, some shrinking of glaciers and ice caps, and an ankle- to calf-high rise of the sea level. Global warming has probably (though this is not provable) contributed to the storm surges off the coasts of Bangladesh and other low-lying countries and the expansion of the range of malarial mosquitoes, increasing the death rate from malaria particularly in Rwanda.

The earth is warming more quickly now. Between 1890 and 1990 the earth's surface temperature increased by 0.3 to 0.6°C. Nine of the ten hottest years on record occurred between 1987 and 1997, and the 1990s were globally the hottest since the fourteenth century.[7]

Scientists may want to point out that these changes are within the range of natural variation. Measurements from phenomena that occur in most parts of the earth, including tree-ring records, borehole temperature measurements in soil, permafrost and ice sheets, and measurements of the mass balance of valley glaciers and ice caps can offer a good overview of the range of temperatures of the earth as a whole (because they can be found all over the world). On the timescale of the last few thousand years there have been larger climatic variations – of the order of 10°C – than those being seen now. It should also be noted that, in the past, increases in temperature have happened when there have not been high levels of carbon dioxide in the atmosphere. However, when there have been large natural variations of carbon dioxide there have always been climatic changes, so there appears to be a relationship, though not demonstrably a causal one.[8]

Whatever the causes, the prospect for the twenty-first century is dramatic, as scientists predict an increase in global warming of between 1 and 5°C, or even higher.[9] Ironically, as air pollution decreases, what may have been a protective layer of soot, smoke and particulate matter will be removed. This may have provided a shield against the effects of global warming during the twentieth century.

Rises in temperature will affect evaporation and precipitation, that is to say, there may be more droughts and more floods. In the UK, for example, summers may be 50 per cent drier and winters up to 30 per cent wetter.[10] Sea levels will rise. Consequences for agriculture will be extreme, and human health will suffer from a greater range of tropical diseases and carriers of disease. Species extinction will accelerate. For some low-lying island nations such as the Maldives or Tuvalu, it could be the final chapter.[11]

Even though it is not possible to pronounce definitively on the causes of global warming, everyone can see the coincidence of massively increased emissions of greenhouse gases into the atmosphere and significant rises in global temperatures. Responses may be different: some may argue that humanity has no chance of reversing the trends of the climate and would serve itself better by preparing for change (moving inland, planting vineyards?). Others will sense the injustice behind the figures: it is the industrialized and industrializing world that is emitting the gases that are affecting the entire planet. The force behind the increase in gas emissions is economic growth. Some may feel that the rich one-third of the world is wealthy enough now, and it is time to share the wealth that, arguably, has been stolen from vulnerable neighbours. A system of bartering 'permits to pollute' which favours the developing world is described in Part Three.

the hydrosphere

Earth is the only place in the solar system where water exists as liquid. There is so much water in the earth – 1.4 billion km³ – that some call it the 'blue planet'. More than 97 per cent of the earth's water is in the oceans. Every year, the sun gathers up about half a million km³, which falls back on to the earth as rain and snow. This is the source of all the world's stock of fresh water. Over two-thirds of it (69 per cent) is currently frozen in ice caps and glaciers, almost all in Antarctica.

Of the 31 per cent that is left, nearly all of it is underground at currently inaccessible depths. Only about one-quarter of one per cent of the world's fresh water (approximately 90,000 km³) is in lakes and rivers where it is accessible. Of this, about a quarter is in Lake Baikal in Siberia. Water is also found in the atmosphere, in permafrost (subsoil that remains frozen throughout the year) and in living organisms.

The renewable stock of water is less than the freshwater stock: about 40,000 km³ per year, which is what is left over after evaporation of rainfall. Of this renewable water, two-thirds runs off in floods. This leaves about 14,000 km³ available for regular use, which divided equally comes to more than 2,000 m³ per person annually. This would be enough, but it is not spread evenly around the world and does not fall at regular intervals. Twenty or thirty countries, mostly in Africa and south-west Asia, have less than half this share per person. South America has ten times as much per person as Asia, and five times as much as Africa. The flow is also unevenly distributed throughout the year, so that many places have either too much or too little water at any one time.[12]

People need water as surely as they need oxygen. For a very long time, humans only needed water to drink. But in the last few thousand years people have also relied upon water to irrigate their crops, carry their wastes, wash their bodies and their possessions and, much more recently, power their mills and machines. Humans used cheap labour and then modern technology to move and control water on vast scales. The twentieth century saw an enormous increase in the use, waste and pollution of water supplies.

water pollution

Historically, humanity has depended upon dilution to control water pollution. This worked for a long time, but as wastes built up through industrialization and urbanization, the method has not been so effective.

For a very long time **rivers** carried off human wastes. With the increase in human numbers and activity, and the greater toxicity of what is dumped, this facility has reached capacity. The story of Oued Fez, a small river in Morocco, is typical of thousands of rivers in the twentieth century.[13] On its way to the Sebou River and the Atlantic Ocean, the Oued Fez flows through the city of Fez, whose population was about 1 million in 1995. Fez's systems for water supply and sewage were built in the tenth century; downstream of the city the water was filthy. The city expanded upstream in the centuries that followed. Industries such as leather tanning and, from 1960, chemical fertilizers from the Sais plain, as well as human waste, polluted the water.

By 1990 the water below the city was 50 times as foul as it had been in the fourteenth century, and carried 5 to 10 times the legal limit of several pollutants.

Inevitably, it is the poorest people who suffer the consequences of river pollution. They must build their houses in the places where no one else will, because that is all they can afford. Poor children bear the heaviest burden of all because they are more vulnerable to the germs the water carries. 'Some estimates attribute up to 80 per cent of illnesses in [Latin America and the Caribbean] and one third of deaths to contaminated water.'[14]

Lakes cannot be flushed out as rivers potentially can. Their biggest threat comes from eutrophication. This happens when unusual quantities of nitrogen or phosphorus appear, and aquatic plants and bacteria grow. Their decomposition consumes oxygen and that threatens the life of other organisms. This process can happen naturally but in the twentieth century it happened more and more as a result of human activity. Small lakes near cities were the first to succumb to the process but now every enclosed area of water is under threat.

Seas, particularly inland seas, are under the same threat as lakes. Larger seas such as the Baltic and the Mediterranean are semi-enclosed, and it takes decades for them to flush out. Meanwhile thousands of rivers continually empty into them. The Baltic Sea is now also seriously under threat from eutrophication[15] as nutrients are washed into it from surrounding farms, land use changes and wetlands disappear. Toxic hydrogen sulphide has formed in the deeper regions of the Baltic, and nearly a third of the bottom area is calculated to be 'dead', that is, there is almost no animal or fish life there.

The **oceans** are not yet so blighted, though some effects of human encroachment are evident, for example in the radical depletion of fish stocks. People think of the oceans as far too vast to suffer much from their activities; however, since 1945 humans have expected them to accommodate growing doses of metals, chemicals, oil and nuclear radiation. This was the thinking of previous generations in relation to rivers and seas: they were too unimaginably huge to be thought of as affected by human activity. It is now known that this is not the case.

taming and exploiting the hydrosphere

The predominant attitude towards water in the nineteenth and twentieth centuries was that it was a massive resource to be exploited. In 1908, Churchill's attitude when looking at the Owen Falls tumbling from Lake Victoria into the Nile was typical:

> So much power running to waste . . . such a lever to control the natural forces of Africa ungripped, cannot but vex and stimulate the imagination. And what fun to make the immemorial Nile begin its journey by diving into a turbine.[16]

World wars and the Great Depression intervened, but in 1946, construction began on the Owen Falls Dam. In 1954, the Nile waters at last dived into turbines. Lake Victoria became a reservoir, and Uganda and eastern Kenya got 150 megawatts of electrical capacity. Lake Victoria and the communities around her then began to suffer from the symptoms of enclosed water systems already discussed.[17]

A great deal has changed in the hydrosphere because of people who felt much the same way as Churchill did. Lenin, Franklin Roosevelt, Nehru, Deng Xiaoping and a host of lesser figures encouraged massive water projects in the USSR, the US, India and China. They had unprecedented technological means at their disposal. To ensure water in the right amounts in the right places at the right times for whatever one wishes to do with it requires hydraulic engineering, one of humankind's oldest sciences. Since 1850, the extent of this science's reach has been so great that the planet's plumbing has been comprehensively reconfigured. In the twentieth century, using ancient and modern methods, several million dams, tubewells, canals, aqueducts and pipelines were built to divert water.

In the distant past, only societies that could concentrate vast armies of labourers could make big changes to the hydrosphere. In the twentieth century, societies with powerful technologies and sufficient wealth could do it. After the waning of colonialism, ambitious governments often seized upon water projects as useful for their domestic and international ends, as in modern India or Egypt, using energy-intensive technology or armies of labourers when needed. Dam building and wetlands drainage reached its height during the decades of the Cold War, when the US and the USSR saw themselves locked in an economic and public relations struggle for which water projects, both within their borders and beyond, seemed most useful.

Economic development and human well-being have depended on successful water projects, but the success may be short-lived. Irrigation has made a big difference to the human condition, but in dry lands it has caused problems as fast as it has solved them. Groundwater use often became groundwater mining, permitting local and regional population and economic expansion while the water lasted. Groundwater mining is now so widespread in south-east Asia in particular that there are fears that the continent is being 'sucked dry'.[18] The straitjacketing of rivers with dams and channels drastically changed habitats in order to make rivers more convenient for human use. Draining wetlands provided more land for people but obliterated the habitats of other species. The physical changes to the hydrological cycle were vast in their consequences for wildlife, for people, for societies and, insofar as the future has been constrained, for posterity as well.[19]

the lithosphere and pedosphere

The *lithosphere* is the outer crust of the earth, some 120 km thick, rock floating on molten rock. The *pedosphere* is the soil that lies on top of the lithosphere like skin on flesh, about half a metre thick and made of a complex mix of many substances including sand, clay, silt and organic matter. It acts like a cleansing and protecting membrane between the lithosphere and the atmosphere.

lithosphere: human geological disturbance

On average the earth's rocks have eroded, deposited on ocean floors as sediment, consolidated into rock again and been thrust up above sea level again 25 times in the history of the earth. By contrast, human impact was minuscule until the industrial age. At that time mining for fossil fuels increased exponentially. A measure of the amount of disturbance is shown by the fact that between 1950 and 1990 mining in the USA affected an area of fertile soil the size of New Jersey (approximately 20,295 km^2).[20]

During the twentieth century humans for the first time moved enough soil and rock to rival natural disturbances. By the 1990s humans were moving 42 billion tons of rock and soil per annum, mainly through mining and accelerated soil cultivation (see below). This is comparable to natural movements such as, for example, the 30 billion tons moved per annum by oceanic volcanoes, or the 4.3 billion tons per annum activated by glacier movement.[21]

pedosphere: cultivation of the soil

Changes to the pedosphere take place continually by means of water and wind. Humans have affected the pedosphere through cultivation of the land as they settled on it. The first wave of human expansion and settlement took place in the Middle East, India and China, when agriculture spread from the river valleys to forest lands, between 2000 BC and AD 1000. As forests were cut down or burned to make way for crops and animals, erosion of the soil resulted, though this stabilized as farms developed.

More significant and potentially damaging effects on the pedosphere took place as Europe expanded, beginning with the Americas after 1492. As populations stabilized between 1650 and 1700, the erosion weakened, but strengthened again around 1840 when some 60 million Europeans migrated to colonial lands. Landscapes whose soil was lighter, whose slopes were steeper, and on which rain fell much more heavily, could not sustain the farming methods of Northern European migrants. These farmers were used to mild rainfall, low slopes and heavy soils resistant to erosion, and many assumed they could import their farming methods on to the more fragile landscapes of the Americas, South Africa, Australasia and Inner Asia. The problems this sort of farming caused were exacerbated by farmers who left fields bare at any time of the year and let their hoofed animals roam freely. Moreover, the power of the European conquerors to shunt native populations around meant that marginal lands came under the plough and digging stick.

In the twentieth century human populations exploded and needed more and more land to settle on and cultivate for food. The 'green revolution' of the 1950s was the name given to the development of ways of feeding a dramatically growing population. These methods included breeding programmes and the use of fertilizers, with sometimes devastating consequences for the soil. At the same time, the US-led integration of the world economic system after 1945 led to the increased cultivation of coffee, citrus fruits, bananas and beef cattle. These claimed fertile tropical lowlands, and subsistence food production once more shifted to marginal lands. Lowland peasants moved to highland regions, mountain peasants invaded rainforests and others colonized semi-arid land.

Ingrained agricultural systems were once again applied in inappropriate settings. Technological developments to serve increased human numbers led to, *inter alia*, soil compaction from the weight of farm machines after 1930 and industrial air pollution. The heavy use of nitrogen fertilizers after 1960 led to the acidification of soils, irrigation encouraged soil salinization, and urbanization and road-building buried soils throughout the twentieth century.

the biosphere

The *biosphere* is the sum of all the habitats in which species live. It includes every home in every part of the world, from the bubbling seafloor vents teeming with bacteria to glaciers at dizzy heights where the occasional beetle may be found, and everything in between. The biosphere is the home of the *biota*, which is the name for all living things, including the human species.

By the twentieth century, for the richer third of the world, the human species was able to dominate all other species as never before. This was due to its ability to feed itself and treat the diseases that had hitherto been fatal. For species other than human, the chances of survival depended on their ability to live within a human-dominated biosphere. There were those organisms that met human needs and were capable of being domesticated, such as cattle, rice and eucalyptus, and they fared well. There were those that found niches within the biosphere, such as rats, crab-grass and the tuberculosis bacillus, and these, too, survived well. Creatures that humans found useful but incapable of domestication, such as blue whales and bison, and those that could not adjust to a human-dominated biosphere, such as gorillas and the smallpox virus, faced extinction. Their survival depended upon whether humans suffered them or not. This 'rogue' human domination is only apparent, however. The changes for which humans have been responsible have for the most part been inadvertent: humans have not intended to wipe out species (apart from some disease-bearing viruses and bacteria), but that is what has happened.

other influences on the biosphere

The heady changes in human health and agriculture, together with more powerful technologies and more tightly integrated markets, encouraged faster and therefore more threatening harvesting of forests and fish in the twentieth century. The other great biological feature of the twentieth century was the extent of bioinvasions, when one creature somehow establishes itself in a new place, thrives and upsets previous balances. Some were deliberate, but the most disruptive were accidental. The most costly in economic terms were the insect pests like the boll weevil from Mexico and the fire ant from Brazil, both of which arrived in the US and wreaked untold havoc on crops. The European rabbit is another example; its most successful invasion was in Australia. It first arrived in 1859; by 1870 it was a pest in much of the country. The resulting erosion of biodiversity may yet prove to be more consequential than either disease control in humans or the revolution in farming.

biological diversity and its loss

It is the very diversity of species that ensures a balance of life on earth, and creates and sustains the circumstances in which life flourishes, including human life. In a thimbleful of earth can be found algae, fungi, nematodes, mites, springtails, enchytraeid worms and thousands of species of bacteria. This is a tiny fragment of one ecosystem. It is a sample of the living force that maintains the earth as a place where life can flourish.

It might be imagined that science and technology will permit humans to create an artificial world in which they can survive as other species fall into extinction around them, a 'literal space ship'.[22] As humans destroy the biological diversity that serves their need for air, light, water, food and shelter, they could try to mimic these services themselves, if that is what is wanted. It is unlikely that humans will succeed in any case, but the fact is that people would not want to live in such an artificial world. Humans grew up with the planet as it is and share its history. People experience nature as profoundly nourishing because it is literally part of what they are. Moreover, 'wilderness settles peace on the soul because it needs no help; it is beyond human contrivance'.[23]

In the light of this, humans who wonder whether it matters if a species becomes extinct are evidence of a mindset that persists in believing that the world is a backdrop to the human story, and the survival of species is relevant only if people happen to like the colour mix. Every scrap of diversity should be judged as priceless unless and until it can be proven that it has no use (the precautionary principle). It should be noted that just existing amounts to a function, because by just being there species are maintaining diversity, and diversity maintains life.

summary and conclusion

Humans have encroached significantly into each of the earth's spheres, on which all living beings depend, and never more so than in the last 100 years. The twentieth century can be seen as a time of tremendous human prodigality, a project of growth without limit. The project has favoured some and hurt far more others. The solution to inequality has been seen as yet more growth, but if humanity cannot restrain its own exuberance it may be that the earth is forced to do it. The evidence in each of the spheres is that a tipping point may be close, when what has been withstood for centuries can be no longer. The sudden changes that would occur in weather systems, the fertility of the soil, the water and the world of living creatures if this tipping point were reached could be devastating.

Even if ecological devastation is not on the horizon, for Christians there must be a recognition that the project of growth without limit has to be curtailed. Furthermore, the injustices spawned by massive growth already exist. Two-thirds of the world does not have enough to eat while the other third is trying to lose weight. There are good reasons to believe that the so-called natural disasters that harm the two-thirds world are part of the consequences of human encroachment on the earth's systems.

The earth is a magnificent place and it is a privilege to be a part of it, but it seems that humanity, unlike other species, has to learn its place. The understanding required in order to do so is not primarily scientific, though science must inform it. Part Two offers some contribution to this understanding, using resources from biblical and theological perspectives.

biblical and theological reflection

In describing the biblical and theological material relevant to environmental issues, Christian insights will be offered as a contribution to the wider discourse. It should also become clear that concern for the creation is fundametal to the Christian faith.

stewards of creation

God created the universe; humans can only hope to adapt it. A Christian understanding of the environment has to start with this fundamental premise. The creation belongs to God, not to humans. The human role is defined as a steward of creation, exercising dominion under God, whose rule is sovereign.

To help understand how this stewardship might be practised, four theological principles will be explored.[1] These are: the covenant with creation; the sacrament of creation; the role of humanity; and the Sabbath. Each section will cover both biblical and theological teachings and insights.

the covenant with creation

After the devastation of the flood that wiped out nearly all life on the planet, God made a covenant with Noah and with every living creature, that he would never again bring about such destruction to the earth (Genesis 9). The nature of this covenant is that it establishes the unbreakable interrelatedness of all creatures and creation itself with their creator God:

> This is the sign of the covenant that I make between you and every living creature that is with you, for all future generations . . . When the bow is in the clouds I will see

it and remember the everlasting covenant between God
and every living creature of all flesh that is on the earth.

Genesis 9.12,16

This covenant with all living things is echoed in Hosea:

And I will make for you a covenant on that day with the
beasts of the field, the birds of the air, and the creeping
things of the ground.

Hosea 2.18

The Hebrew word for covenant, *berit'*, shares a root with the word used
in Genesis to describe divine creativity, *bara*. This root conveys the
sense of binding. Through God's gracious love, creation is bound by the
everlasting covenant to the invisible God, and all creatures are bound to
each other in a web of interrelationship. The creation was established in
a divinely intended state of 'shalom', meaning peace, justice, harmony
and integrity. It is good and seen by God as good (Genesis 1). Passages
in Isaiah 11, 24, 32 and 55 as well as a number of Psalms (e.g. 89 and
104) describe or convey this integrity and connectedness of all things
with God and with each other. This is the case when the covenant bonds
are held together and when they are broken: either way, everything is
affected. These passages also teach that the covenant establishes
moral responsibilities of human beings to each other and to the whole
created order.

In Jesus Christ, the covenant is renewed:

When anyone is in Christ there is a new creation.

2 Corinthians 5.17

At the beginning of John's Gospel it is made plain that all things were
made through him and all things find their fulfilment in him. Through
the incarnation, death and resurrection it can be learned that to be
fully human is to be in communion with God and know him as the
creator of humanity along with the rest of the created order.

The image of the covenant as a spider's web is instructive: each of its
strands supports the whole. If just one or two strands of the web are
cut, the web may survive, sever enough strands and the whole web falls
apart. This biblical insight into the nature of things is reflected in the
empirical observations of biologists. E. O. Wilson demonstrates that

sustaining the earth happens by virtue of biological diversity: the earth depends on all beings in all their different ways, all together at once.

> Biological diversity . . . is the key to the maintenance of the world as we know it. Life in a local site struck down by a passing storm springs back quickly because enough diversity still exists. Opportunistic species evolved for just such an occasion rush in to fill the spaces. They entrain the succession that circles back to something resembling the original state of the environment.
>
> But the restorative power of the fauna and flora of the world as a whole depends on the existence of enough species to play that special role. They too can slide into the red zone of endangered species.[2]

Hildegard of Bingen echoed the same perception of interdependence when she wrote: 'God has made all things in the world in consideration of everything else.'

By contrast, the perception that separates human beings from the environment in which they developed is fundamentally mistaken. Living beings did not find their abode on the earth and then adapt to it. Rather, the environment and organisms evolved together, so that it is not really possible to separate them and think of one existing despite the other, or as a tenant of the other, or on the face of the other. Humanity is a part of a glorious, diverse whole. One of the great challenges of feminist theology to Christians is to 'join the mess' rather than try to escape it or impose an artificial framework upon it.[3]

Many people find themselves deeply refreshed by being in touch with nature. Olivier Clement describes how Jung would return to a favourite place near Lake Zurich and live a simple life close to nature: 'he prepared his own wood, lit the fire, went to the spring for water, and sat in the light of a living flame'. He saw himself 'in each tree, in the lapping of the waves, in the clouds, in the animals that came and went, in objects'.[4]

Evelyn Underhill describes the first stage of contemplation as a means to connect with any or all things in creation, and coming to understand how related everything is:

Stretch out by a distinct act of loving will towards one of the myriad manifestations of life that surround you: and which, in an ordinary way, you hardly notice unless you happen to need them . . . All things in this world towards which you are stretching out are linked together, and one truly apprehended will be the gateway to the rest . . . Old barriers will vanish; and you will become aware that St Francis was accurate as well as charming when he spoke of Brother Wind and Sister Water.[5]

The human body is made of the same matter as the rest of creation, and is constantly exchanging particles with it. Humanity cannot be understood as separate even at the physical level. A way of experiencing this unity of the elements is to connect with each of the senses in turn, for each of the senses is related to a particular element (smell to earth; taste to water; sight to fire; and touch to air). Engaging in such an exercise demonstrates human connectedness to everything else, and the striving to maintain a separate (and usually fearful) existence apart from the rest of God's creation ceases.

This is not a call to earth-worship. It is a recognition of the unbreakable kinship of all God's creatures. It points to the underlying unity of all things and if that can be connected with, then there is a connection with the cosmic Christ because his body is the whole universe.[6]

He is the image of the invisible God, the first-born of all creation; for in him all things were created, in heaven and on earth, visible and invisible, whether thrones or dominions or principalities or authorities – all things were created through him and for him. He is before all things, and in him all things hold together.

Colossians 1.15-17

Christ redeems the whole creation, and his power of life over death means that there is not one scrap of the universe that will not be part of the new creation.[7]

The covenant with creation is the acknowledgement of the total interdependence and connectedness of every part of the creation, brought forth from the one God. Humanity stands apart from the rest of creation in this respect: it can understand this relationship, and can express it and renew it in the form of love.

the sacrament of creation

In the person of the Holy Spirit, God is continually sustaining the whole creation with divine energy and potentiality. God knows and counts every minute movement of the comprehensively diverse creation in which not even two blades of grass are the same as each other. Everything is unique, and everything is a vehicle of God's self-expression by which God speaks from within (Psalm 148.5; Hebrews 1.3). It follows that no part of the creation can be thought of as outside God's grace and there is nowhere called 'away' where things can be thrown. The sacredness of creation and the unifying Wisdom that shines through it all is recognized, as the extent of its diversity is seen and appreciated.

Mother Julian wrote:

> See, I am God: see, I am in all things: see, I do all things: see, I never lift my hands off my works, nor ever shall, without end: see, I lead all things to the end that I ordain it to, from without-beginning, by the same might, wisdom and love that I made it with. How should anything be amiss?[8]

This detailed and unitary appreciation opens up a world that is lively and responsive, as Jacques Lusseyran, a Frenchman blinded at the age of eight and learning how to function in the world without the use of his eyes, discovered through pressure:

> If I put my hand on the table without pressing it, I knew the table was there, but knew nothing about it. To find out, my fingers had to bear down, and the amazing thing is that the pressure was answered by the table at once. Being blind, I thought I should have to go out to meet things, but I found that they came to meet me instead.[9]

True blindness is failing to recognize the exquisite, lively uniqueness of every part of God's creation as an expression of God. Anne Primavesi encourages people to see themselves as members of the biological community, together and individually revealing 'Godself'.[10] If the beauty of this diversity-in-community is not seen, then it is not valued and will not be 'kept', as Adam was commanded:

The Lord God took the man and put him in the garden of
Eden to till it and keep it.

Genesis 2.15

Eco-feminist Heather Eaton writes: 'If . . . the natural world [is] invisible
in our education, [its] destruction will be as well.'[11]

The loss of biological diversity should be equivalent in a person's mind
with the loss of very great works of art. Every kind of organism has
reached this moment against nearly impossible odds, inching its way
out of an ancient history of evolution and development which humanity
shares. 'Such is the ultimate and cryptic truth of every kind of organism,
large and small, every bug and weed. The flower in the crannied wall –
it *is* a miracle.'[12]

A contemporary ascetic quoted by Bartholomew I, the 'Green Patriarch',
points out that the veneration of clothing that had been worn by a saint
was a common practice. 'Is it not much more fitting,' he asks, 'that we
should also venerate the flowers and the plants? After all, they enshrine
within themselves the energy of God.'[13]

the role of humanity

Misguided anthropocentrism has had unfortunate effects both on the
earth and on humanity itself. The human species, as a result, can be
and is seen as irrelevant at best, and at worst a terrible calamity for life
on earth, a rogue species of rapacious bipeds bent on destruction. But
this self-abnegation and false modesty are equally mistaken perceptions
and can just as easily lead to destructive behaviour. 'We are treating our
environment, our planet, in an inhuman, godforsaken manner precisely
because we see it in this way, precisely because we see ourselves in
this way.'[14]

What, then, is the proper place of humanity on the planet? The Bible
offers three roles: prophets, priests and kings.[15]

A **prophet** is a seer: one who perceives things as they truly are, that
is, shown by God, and who speaks of what he or she sees.

When a person looks at the world as independent, objective and
separate from its creator, s/he is like the prodigal son who takes

his share of the universe and turns his back on his maker. After he has finished investigating it and using it for himself he is left with the empty husk of old knowledge, knowing that there is something missing, the most important thing, which is *not* his material well-being.

The prophet sees to the inner essence of each and every thing, and stands witness to its reality. He sees the *logos* of God, which made the thing come to be, as the Psalmist declared: 'He spoke, and they came to be; he commanded, and they were created' (Psalm 148.5), and the letter to the Hebrews affirms: 'He upholds all things by the word of his power' (Hebrews 1.3). Every part of the creation is given its unique role in the cosmic symphony by this word of God,[16] and it is separately counted, as the Gospel tells us: 'even the hairs of your head are all numbered' (Matthew 10.30; Luke 12.7). This inner sight is what artists connect with and then try to portray, and it is what blind Jacques Lusseyran saw.

To be a prophet is to be primarily receptive. Simone Weil said:

> Attention consists of suspending our thought, leaving it detached, empty, and ready to be penetrated by the object . . . Above all our thought should be empty, waiting, not seeking anything, but ready to receive in its naked truth the object that is to penetrate it . . . The love of our neighbour in all its fullness simply means being able to say to him: 'What are you going through?' . . . This way of looking is first of all attentive. The soul empties itself of all its own contents in order to receive into itself the being it is looking at, just as he is, in all his truth.[17]

Once the prophet sees, s/he stands in awe. When asked what he was doing in a place, a monk simply said, 'Keeping it'.[18] The prophet understands the power of silent observation. Intelligent contemplation of things as they really are, restraining the urge to experiment, interfere, change or improve, is a service humanity can offer the whole created order, and its effects cannot be underestimated. What is seen is understood, and what is understood is loved. If no time is made simply to see what is, it will not be missed until it has gone for ever, and then it will be too late. Starets Zosima says in *The Karamazov Brothers*:

Love all of God's creation, love the whole, and love each grain of sand. Love every leaf, every ray of God's light. Love animals, love plants, love every kind of thing. If you love every kind of thing, then everywhere God's mystery will reveal itself to you. Once this has been revealed to you, you will begin to understand it ever more deeply with each passing day. And finally you will be able to love the whole world with an all-encompassing universal love.[19]

Once s/he sees, the prophet must speak. Christ exemplified this. His programme of work, as declared in Luke 4, can be understood in a way that is directly relevant to this theme:

The spirit of the Lord is upon me, because he has anointed me to preach good news to the poor. He has sent me to proclaim release to the captives and recovering of sight to the blind, to set at liberty those who are oppressed, to proclaim the acceptable year of the Lord.

Luke 4.18-19

It is a prophetic role to speak of the beauty and goodness of the creation; to make people see things as they really are; and to free the earth (in this context) from the oppression of exploitation, ignorance and plunder.

The **priest** is primarily active. Zizioulas has noted how human beings are challenged and provoked by the givenness of creation. It is very hard for human beings simply to adapt to their environment; something in them wants to change it rather than themselves, perhaps because they can. Humans want to 'pass everything that exists through their hands'[20] and call it their own. People can do this for their own benefit; this would be to exercise dominion in a utilitarian way in which the human being believes him or herself to be godlike and at the same time cuts him or herself off from nature, which becomes merely the means by which self-satisfaction and pleasure are attained. Humans can engage with creation less ambitiously, seeking only to meet the basic needs for clothing, shelter and food. This would be to exercise dominion in a personal way, but has no meaning beyond itself.

However, humanity may choose to pass creation through its hands in order to transform it, acting as God's servants, and this is to become a priest of creation. Standing between earth and heaven, the priest can bring God's blessing on all the earth, by caring for it as God's steward, not its master. The priest's hands become God's hands, and through him what is touched is transformed. For some, this is most clearly demonstrated in the eucharistic feast. The elements of earthly reality, the bread and wine, become a means of grace for human beings and also themselves receive new meaning and status as they are offered to God. The offertory prayer acknowledges the balance between what has been given by God and what part humanity has played in transforming it:

> Blessed are you, Lord God of all creation: through your goodness we have this bread to set before you, which earth has given and human hands have made. It will become for us the bread of life.

By developing and using the earthly gifts of God rightly, human beings accept and help them to realize their potential as communicators of God's reality. This is a microcosm of the priestly role in relation to the earth as a whole. Human beings should transform nature with the understanding that it is a gift from God, knowing that once the transformation is effected, the creation must be offered back to God. Icon painters in the Orthodox tradition enable the earthly elements of wood and egg tempera, varnish and gold leaf to serve God by being instrumental in the creation of holy icons. Thereby, 'creation becomes fully articulate in praise of God'.[21] The Transfiguration is another example of this transformation of the material world, in which the spun linen of Christ's robe participated in his uncreated light.

Christ is the supreme exemplar of the priestly role. As priests, human beings have the choice to live sacramentally, receiving all creation as a gift, transforming it and returning it to God, or to live selfishly, separating creation from its source and accruing it to themselves exclusively.

> When we [work in the world] knowingly, lovingly, skilfully and reverently it is a sacrament. When we do it ignorantly, greedily and destructively it is a desecration. In such a desecration we condemn ourselves to spiritual and moral loneliness and others to want.[22]

The third human role is that of **kingship**. The servant-king defends the rights of the poor and disadvantaged; for example:

It is not for kings, O Lemuel,
it is not for kings to drink wine,
or for rulers to desire strong drink;
lest they drink and forget what has been decreed,
and pervert the rights of all the afflicted.
Give strong drink to him who is perishing,
and wine to those in bitter distress;
let them drink and forget their poverty,
and remember their misery no more.
Open your mouth for the dumb,
for the rights of all who are left desolate.
Open your mouth, judge righteously,
maintain the rights of the poor and needy.

Proverbs 31.4-9

Kingship also implies dominion:

And God blessed them, and God said to them, 'Be fruitful and multiply, and fill the earth and subdue it; and have dominion over the fish of the sea and over the birds of the air and over every living thing that moves upon the earth.'

Genesis 1.28

A wrong understanding of human dominion over the earth has had devastating consequences. What might the proper meaning of the verse be? Does it imply, if not tyrannical lordship, at the very least some sort of pivotal leadership role in relation to the earth? Does the earth depend on humans in any way?

According to Romans 8, Christians are key to the salvation of the earth:[23]

I consider that the sufferings of this time are not worth comparing to the glory that is to be revealed to us. For the creation waits with eager longing for the revealing of the sons of God; for the creation was subjected to futility (nothingness, going nowhere), not of its own will, but by the will of him who subjected it in hope; because the creation itself will be set free from its bondage to decay and obtain the glorious liberty of the children of God.

Romans 8.18-21

Irenaeus understands this passage to mean that the earth will put forth a superabundance of fertility:

> The predicted blessing, therefore, belongs unquestionably to the times of the kingdom, when the righteous shall bear rule upon their rising from the dead; when also the creation, having been renovated and set free, shall fructify with an abundance of all kinds of food.
>
> [Quoting Papias] 'The days will come when vineyards will grow, each having ten thousand shoots and in one shoot ten thousand branches . . . and upon every sprig ten thousand clusters, and in every cluster ten thousand grapes, and every grape when pressed shall yield twenty-five measures of wine. Every grain of wheat would yield huge quantities of flour, fruit trees and grass would flourish and all animals would live at peace with each other.'[24]

Isaiah 65 describes at length a picture of restored right relationships in the 'new heaven and new earth'.

How are the children of God to bring this about? Paul provides the answer. Christ, he says in 1 Corinthians 15, is the second Adam. The role to which the first Adam was called and failed to fulfil, the role to which Christ and the children of God that follow him are now called, was to 'till and keep' the garden (Genesis 2.15). This is the kingly role, the exercise of dominion for humanity to fulfil, commanded of Adam before the Fall and prophesied by Isaiah:

> In days to come Jacob shall take root,
> Israel shall blossom and put forth shoots,
> and fill the whole world with fruit.
>
> Isaiah 27.6

Dominion is an exercise of vicegerency: lordship under God. The biblical term for humanity's relationship with creation is 'steward'. A steward is a servant who relates to God, on whose behalf s/he exercises dominion. S/he is also called to render an account to God of his/her stewardship of tilling and keeping.

the Sabbath feast of enoughness

> Then the heavens and the earth were finished, and all the host of them. And on the seventh day God finished his work which he had done, and he rested on the seventh day from all his work which he had done. So God blessed the seventh day and hallowed it, because on it God rested from all his work which he had done in creation.
>
> Genesis 2.1-3

The Sabbath, in which all things come to rest, is the fourth and final principle to consider. It is the Sabbath, established on the seventh day, not humanity on the sixth, that is the crown of creation.[25] It was the day in which God himself took a rest, and there is no suggestion that he did so because he was tired.

Humankind is easily ensnared in the culture of ownership. Even if it is understood intellectually that the world is God's and the human role of stewardship means to have dominion only under him, people can still find themselves caught by desire, which is by its nature voracious. The desire to have possessions can consume a person's waking hours and even his/her sleep in dreams. In the midst of this, the Christian is called to stop: completely, properly, for a period of time. Not just to pause for breath before carrying on consuming, but to take a deep dive into God's peace. A regular practice of silence should be welcomed, because it offers the opportunity to experience freedom from the demands of a consumer society, rather than just to think that it would be a good idea.

The bow and arrow can serve as an analogy. The further back the bow is drawn into the depths of God, the further and more truly the arrow will fly to serve justice and peace when it is then let loose into the world. The greater the inner nourishment that comes from God alone, the fewer the demands will be on the material world for personal satisfaction. Meditation reduces ecological footprints. When it is known for a fact, because it is regularly experienced, that the most important thing is not material, not external, cannot be bought with money or bartered for with anything that a person has, when it is known that the only way to reach that unbelievably special place is precisely by putting down everything a person believes he/she is and owns, his/her faith in the capacity of the material world to bring him/her lasting satisfaction is utterly undermined.

> I must give all that I have
> to possess it. Life is not hurrying
> on to a receding future, nor hankering after
> an imagined past. It is the turning
> aside like Moses to the miracle
> of the lit bush, to a brightness
> that . . . is the eternity that awaits you.[26]

When his/her eyes open after a period and contemplate what is before them from the divine love that may have touched him/her, s/he knows that s/he is not different from the world, and to harm the world, to touch it harshly, to ignore it or to claim it, is to harm him/herself.

> I have been dipped again in God, and new-created.[27]

The Sabbath is an occasion of thanksgiving, a feast of contentment and 'enoughness'.[28] In the Sabbath rhythm of days and years, passing time is given a measure and the earth is given a rest. The fallow season constrains human activity and limits human exploitation of both the natural order and of the poor. Leaving land fallow and forgiving debts are part of the Jubilee call to justice and peace. Every seventh year the crops and fruit trees must be left unharvested and unpruned, so that there is food for the poor (Exodus 23.10, Leviticus 25.1-7). Every seventh day is given over to rest and refreshment (Exodus 23.12), particularly for servants and aliens.[29] Sabbath requires a letting go. Those who tried hoarding the manna given by God in the wilderness found that it bred maggots and stank. 'It is this stink which rises today from all over our despoiled environment.'[30]

Finally, there is the question of what might be called the ultimate Sabbath: the last days. Some Christians have taken 2 Peter 3.10 to mean that the end of the world will take the form of a final and devastating conflagration. There is one school of thought that proposes that this day is nearly upon us, for the earth is unquestionably warming up, and that Christians must do what they can to speed up the process by burning as many fossil fuels as possible. That way their final salvation will happen sooner rather than later, sinners will be left to burn up, and the earth can go hang. But as James Jones has pointed out, fire is not only an agent of destruction but also one of purification or refinement: 'Peter's reference to fire suggests to me a cataclysmic event of purification in the process of waiting "for new heavens and a new earth, where righteousness is at home" (2 Peter 3.13).'[31]

part three

a practical Christian response

introduction

For active, caring human beings, the response to reading the above is very likely to be one of asking the question, 'What can I do?' But the very first question is not about doing, but about being, or rather perceiving. A proper understanding of the global environment will bring about a profound change in perception, such that actions and behaviours will become quite obviously appropriate or inappropriate. So the very first Christian response in seeking to care for creation is to see what is happening. Perceiving aright requires a change of heart or mind, the literal meaning of the word *metanoia*, translated as repentance. Weighing in too fast with solutions to the world's problems has caused untold damage in the past, and a Christian has to be sure that his/her responses are appropriate before trying to do too much. The energy needed to change lifestyles and consumer decisions comes from the repentance of a change of heart and from prayer. There are exercises and discussion topics on pages 39–41 to help effect a change in perception.

sustainable consumption

Of course, living in itself involves innumerable decisions and actions, and these can be carried out in ways that reduce or even reverse damage to the environment. *Sustainable consumption* is the phrase that has been coined to describe this way of living. The last 100 years show just how influential consumer choice has been.[1]

Consider the attitudes to clothing of the leisured classes. Clothes that were as conspicuously expensive as they could be commanded respect. Clothes that had a built-in obsolescence also commanded respect – that is, a dress was worn once and then cast aside, even though it was in perfectly good condition. After the Second World War, advertising, supported by vanity and avarice, created a new 'good' out of branding.

Producers and retailers will maximize the preferences of the consumer in an economically optimum way. They will not usually, unless the consumer wants them to, consider the ethical implications of how they obtain their produce, how it travels and in what form it is sold. There are brave exceptions to this rule, such as the Body Shop, which has succeeded in persuading consumers to consider the ethics of their choices. Churches have also been pioneers with their stalls selling fairly traded products. Thanks to such ethical behaviour, attitudes are changing more generally, and even the supermarkets are being forced to change, albeit too slowly.

The fundamental point is that each person has to take account of the impact that his or her consuming decisions have on the whole world order, environmental, social and economic, and of his/her responsibility to give an account to God of the way in which s/he has used the gifts God has given.

ecological footprints

An effective and imaginative way of considering human use and impact on the environment is to think of it in terms of 'footprints'. A person's impact (footprint) on the earth is greatest in the industrialized Western countries. Can such a footprint be reduced? Is the size of a person's impact on the earth morally and ecologically defensible? The definition of a nation's or a person's 'ecological footprint' is the biologically productive area needed to produce the resources used and absorb the waste generated by that person or nation. To gain a sense of the comparative footprints of citizens of different countries, the average Polish citizen's is 3.7 hectares, and the average Finnish citizen's is 8.4.[2] The web site www.myfootprint.org helps individuals to calculate their own footprints. Friends of the Earth has done important work in this area and more information can be found on their web site: www.foe.org.

sustainable development

The challenges facing the earth have to be met holistically. It is widely recognized that only to respond to environmental concerns without considering the social or economic implications is too narrow to be truly helpful; in the same way, in the end, it does not work to deal only with social or economic injustice without considering the environment. The phrase *sustainable development* has been coined to cover all three aspects of universal well-being: social, economic and environmental. Sustainable development means 'enjoying the earth's resources without jeopardizing future generations'.[3]

Sustainable development is not an easy concept for anyone to comprehend and put into practice. It is so all-encompassing. Non-Governmental Organizations (NGOs) have been working hard to try to develop more holistic approaches to the world's problems, but it is still the case that development NGOs regard environment NGOs with suspicion, and vice versa, each assuming the other does not properly understand 'their' issues. A nation, or even a group of nations, ultimately responsible for its own citizens' interests, will not usually look beyond itself to the needs of those who are not citizens but are nevertheless part of humanity, except out of self-interest. A company, answerable to its shareholders for profit, will not automatically serve a wider community or environment. The very nature of the different institutions and organizations militates against such attitudes and approaches. They have been created to serve particular interests and stakeholders, specific needs and aspirations. Not serving those particulars undermines their very *raison d'être*.

There is, of course, a long tradition of NGOs and nations trying to work together for mutual benefit or around specific issues such as peace, trade and, more recently, climate change. But the bartering necessary to achieve agreement to even small changes among nations is slow and highly complex (for example, the Kyoto Protocol). For not only institutions, but also people, find it difficult to break out of established approaches to problems, in short, to be paradigm-busters.

Christians should not suffer from such narrow self-interest. The Christian's *raison d'être* is the transcendent and immanent divine, so s/he cannot tie him/herself to one thing in this world more than another. The Christian's home is both everywhere in the whole world, and not in the world at all, and the Christian's family is all humanity. Christians are thus well placed to support holistic responses to global problems.

To meet the needs of the world holistically, complexity has to be accepted and the wider context borne in mind when taking action. Some case studies are offered to demonstrate what this means. These are a mixture of local projects from the UK and elsewhere, and projects that attempt a global response to global concerns. They are not offered as faultless solutions, but rather as honest attempts to help make the world a better place for people and their environment.

protecting La Moya ecological reserve

The project of Paz y Esperanza (Peace and Hope, an organization supported by Tearfund) to protect La Moya ecological reserve and the communities that depend upon it is recorded here in full in order to convey the many-layered complexity involved in implementing sustainable development.

Ayaviri is a Quechua-speaking community of 17,000 people, situated at an altitude of 4,000 metres in the Andes, Peru. It is centred around an ecological reserve with a lake, called La Moya. This is the only place in the district that remains green all the year round; it also has important historical and cultural significance. Two indigenous communities, descended from the Incas, live on the edge of La Moya and share it with the rest of the Ayaviri. The two communities (Umasyo and Ccapacc Hacco) are considered to be the proprietors of the reserve, but in reality the land is owned by the government.

The communities keep animals in the surrounding fields and, during the dry season (April to June), they are dependent on La Moya for feeding them. However, for many years, La Moya has started to be degraded and is now polluted and under threat of disappearing or being of limited use due to contamination. The reasons for the degradation are that people from the town dump their rubbish in La Moya; running water is only available in the town for a few hours a day so people from there use detergents to wash their clothes in La Moya; people come for sports; the village is on a slope above the lake so that its rubbish and dirty water, including blood from an abattoir, flow into La Moya; and La Moya is used by animals in the dry season. Requests for help from the town's mayor to alleviate this pressure by the two communities have fallen on deaf ears.

Pastor Eron Quispe of the Biblical Institute of Ayaviri started a programme to raise awareness about La Moya in 1999. This involved many-layered work because of leadership changes and mutual distrust between the two communities. The Institute has built strategic alliances with Paz y Esperanza, the Archaeological Museum, and a special body called Mesa de Concertacion, which facilitates consultation and communication with all local groups and institutions. The work of these alliances in education and advocacy led to a decree in 2001 from the mayor to prohibit the dumping of litter in La Moya. The lake is cleaner and people's awareness of the problems is greater, but there are wider infrastructure issues that have to be addressed before the fundamental causes of the damage can be removed. These include providing more running water and drinking water; relocating rubbish sites; re-directing the polluted water and blood from the village away from La Moya; cleaning the lake itself and offering an alternative venue for sports, especially the bull run.

The two indigenous communities have been open to manipulation and discrimination and have had little participation in discussions about the future of the area. They are suspicious of the local authorities and feel threatened. A proposal for a new museum in the area is not helping, because fundamental needs have not been addressed first.

The Biblical Institute plans to work with Mesa de Concertacion to ensure that all communities are included in decisions about the area; to build relationships itself with the communities; to continue the awareness-raising programme; to mobilize individual members of the church; and to work with the authorities to ensure a scientific technical assessment is made of the problems with La Moya.

Taken from a briefing by Graham Gordon of Tearfund, April 2002

environmental audits

In his June 2004 lecture on the environment, the Archbishop of Canterbury called on the Church to undertake an audit of its green credentials[4] and reiterated this call at St Paul's Cathedral on 21 September 2004. It is important that the Church ensures its own house is in order as it seeks to engage with the world in this work. The project *Eco-Congregation* (see Part Four) offers a straightforward and undemanding toolkit for churches to use to undertake an audit and then to improve their ecological track records. Stories from churches that have begun the Eco-Congregation process are inspiring, indicating that this work can bring a church back to life and root it firmly in its local community:

> *We were already committed to environmental concerns through the successful award of a Christian Ecology Link Millennium Certificate when we decided to opt in to Eco-Congregation's audit process. We decided to continue with our aluminium can recycling scheme, raising new money for church funds through the sale of the cans and the recycling of fabrics to help support Derby's Padley Day Centre for the Homeless and its own recycling scheme. We also collect stamps for the local canal restoration society who hope to restore the Derby and Sandiacre Canal which runs right by our church. We continue with our annual litter pick along the canal path – a good way to involve the local community and sympathetic organizations like Derby Cycling Group and The Canal Society. We became a Fair Trade Church recognized by the City Council as a result of our previous commitment to Traidcraft. We still have a long way to go and there is always more that can be done – but we feel we have made a start and there has certainly been a shift in attitude among the majority of church members.*
>
> Revd Donald McDonald, Diocesan Environment Officer
> for Derby Diocese, and vicar of St Osmund's Church, Derby

parish pumps

Often a church starts down this path of environmental engagement because one of its members is an enthusiastic champion and has the energy and commitment necessary to persuade his or her fellow churchgoers. The Conservation Foundation (see Part Four) has a register of some 3,000 such local champions, called 'Parish Pumps' in honour of the place that the pump used to have in each parish: a source of water and a place to gather to learn local news and enjoy one's community. The Parish Pump receives a regular newsletter with stories, information, sources of funding and ideas for projects. Parish Pumps can also apply for 'pump-priming' grants from the Conservation Foundation to fund local activities:

> A large crowd of villagers from Cleeve Prior, near Evesham, joined the Bishop of Dudley when he visited the site of a proposed Parish Sanctuary to present a Parish Pump Priming Award of £700 to the organizers. The half-acre site is being developed from an old enclosed allotment known as Booby's Close, surrounded by hedges, some of which are known to be at least four hundred years old. The project aims to create a haven for wildlife which is also sacred: a special place where local people and visitors can relax, rest and meditate in an environment of peace and calm. The award is being used to cover the cost of installing bird hides, planting areas with native wildflowers and establishing a nursery for native elms.

David Shreeve, Director of the Conservation Foundation

a city's attempt to become more environmental

A good example of civic engagement with environmental issues can be found in Newcastle (web site www.carbonneutralnewcastle.com). The City Council has numerous initiatives to encourage city dwellers to live in more eco-friendly ways. Individuals can only go so far in trying to live ethically if the institutions and environments in which they are active do not support their efforts. This Council's move to meet individual efforts halfway will help ensure that people's motivation is sustained.

contraction and convergence

A global response to climate change called 'contraction and convergence' has been devised by the Global Commons Institute. *Contraction* refers to the movement towards a formal stabilization target of emissions that is sustainable – 60 per cent reduction by 2050 is the widely accepted suggestion; *convergence* is the division of the total contracted carbon emissions by head of population. Each nation would have its carbon emission quota according to the size of its population.

On a per capita basis, countries would be allocated their share of permits to pollute. Post-industrialized countries emit far more greenhouse gases than those of the developing world, and yet have much smaller populations. The richer countries can buy permits to pollute from the poorer countries and thereby offer them much-needed development aid. Contraction and convergence is a simple and radical solution, but a completely global and holistic one, one that requires minds and hearts to be open to the whole world community, rather than the own interests of individual nations or groups of nations. For more information, go to www.gci.org.uk.

Operation Noah

This global solution to climate change and poverty is one that has to be implemented by governments, but it is the willingness of the 'world's mind' to think in this holistic way that will give governments permission to do so. Democratically elected governments can only move as fast as the people who elected them. If the people demonstrate their desire for such global solutions to be implemented, the world's governments will have to follow. Christian Ecology Link (see Part Four) has launched a campaign called Operation Noah by which individuals can lobby the government to support contraction and convergence, and also sign themselves up to a green energy source. This is an excellent example of connecting the global with the local.

some ideas for parish congregations

(Material for these suggestions can be obtained from the organizations listed in Part Four.)

Church buildings and grounds	Community-orientated	Spiritual
Undertake an environmental/energy audit	Environmental project with school	Use of creation-focused prayers and hymns in worship
Install heat conservation measures and change lighting to low-energy sources	Initiate a litter pick in a local 'grot spot'	Special creation care service – sometimes with members of local environmental organizations
Promote sustainable transport e.g. through provision of secure cycle-storage facilities and car sharing	Plant trees in an appropriate locality	Integration of environmental issues into special services, e.g. Harvest Festival
Make/purchase and install bird and bat boxes and bird feeding stations in church grounds	Promote fair trade through a church purchasing policy and by offering fairly traded products for sale	Holding a creation care series of Bible studies
Establish a recycling programme for church consumables such as paper	Establish a recycling point to collect items such as stamps, mobile phones, used printer cartridges, aluminium foil/ cans, shoes	Exploring creation care issues in children's Sunday activities
Initiate a policy at church of using washable crockery and cutlery and environmentally friendly cleaning products	Work with building users on environmental issues	Holding a holiday or summer club with a creation care theme
Switch to green electricity	Undertake practical conservation work	Publishing creation care prayers
Establish a wildlife garden – e.g. through provision of habitats such as hedges and log piles, wildlife feeding and nesting sites	Encourage individuals to adopt a greener lifestyle through articles in church or parish magazines	Using natural materials in worship, e.g. organic bread and wine
Establish and maintain an Environmental Notice Board	Promote activities and achievements through the local media	A prayer walk/pilgrimage/ ramble including faith reflections
Install a compost pit for waste flowers and other organic material and a water butt	Promote and distribute household environmental/ energy audits and water hippos	Choose to dedicate in worship items such as trees prior to planting, recycling containers or low-energy light bulbs
Advertise or provide clear signage of church policy and why it has been initiated	Support/adopt an environmental charity	Include publications or other resources with a creation care focus in any library that the church has
Undertake a wildlife survey in the churchyard	Organize an environmental event/seminar/meeting/ speaker and advertise it in the community (could be during One World Week)	Research, plan and plant a garden using biblical plants/images

subjects for reflection and group discussion[5]

see yourself as a citizen of the planet
- Questions of poverty and environment are distorted if seen only in local or national terms.

waste-watching

Where you have a choice:

- Resist obsolescence; choose the longer-lasting
- Support public transport with your feet and your vote
- Resist wasteful packaging
- See your discarded items not as waste but as sources of new life

work out your way of life

(The web site www.carboncalculator.org may be helpful here.)

Ask such questions as:

- How can we measure our real needs (by the standards of our neighbours or by the needs of the poor)?
- How can we be joyful without being greedy or flamboyant (e.g. in hospitality)?
- How far does our personal way of life depend on *society's* wealth? Can our society's way of life be made simpler? Can we ourselves work for any such change?
- How can we be good stewards without being over-scrupulous? What decisions about personal life are the decisive ones to make (e.g. budgeting)?
- How can others benefit from what we have (our home, our car and other possessions)?

points to ponder
- Happiness is knowing what I can do without
- My greed is another's need
- Am I detached from worldly goods if I keep what I have and want to add to them?
- How in practice can I give an account to God of my stewardship of his creation?
- 'Not my world, but his'
- Question your own lifestyle, not your neighbour's

an exercise in contemplation

Find a quiet place where you will not be disturbed for a period. Your attitude is one of self-sacrifice, and this begins with the sacrifice of time and other worldly commitments. Sit with your eyes closed and your body still and upright. Take some time to find a comfortable but upright position. When your body is still and at rest, watch the movements of your mind, and allow all the thoughts that are passing just to pass. See them as being like traffic, just passing through. Don't latch on to any of them, but don't try and exclude them either. Let them, and everything else that is happening outside, just be. Rest there, without adding anything, just allowing everything for at least ten minutes. You are like Mary, who was content to wait on the Lord. 'Be it unto me according to Thy word' (Luke 1.38).

Now gently let your attention rise up and outwards. Open your eyes. Contemplate what is before them from the divine love that may have touched you.

exercises to help connect with the different elements of God's creation

air and touch

When you next find yourself walking, feel the air on your face, become aware of your breathing, and realize the total and automatic dependence of the life of your body on the atmosphere. Gain a sense of 'being breathed' rather than the other way around. See how the air is one thing: wind, breath, invisibly supporting, moving and enlivening all things.

Become aware that this same atmosphere is warming up and that for some living things, human, animal and plant, the twenty-first century will see the final destruction of their habitats and their livelihoods.

> 'The wind blows where it wills, and you hear the sound of
> it, but you do not know whence it comes or whither it goes;
> so it is with everyone who is born of the Spirit.'
>
> John 3.8

fire and sight

If you can find some fire, watch how it warms and lights, but also burns and destroys. See too how it purges. Become aware of its magnificent power. Consider the energy it has given humanity. Appreciate the light and warmth that brings comfort to your life.

Appreciate the destructive force of burning, as energy is produced and consumed, to make the planet fevered, perhaps beyond what it can endure. Think of your own body's response to a high temperature.

> Fire goes before him, and consumes his adversaries on every side. His lightings light up the world, the earth sees and trembles.
>
> Psalm 97.3-4

> Each man's work will become manifest; for the Day will disclose it, because it will be revealed with fire, and the fire will test what sort of work each one has done.
>
> 1 Corinthians 3.13

water and taste

When you next do something involving water, such as drinking a glass of it, watering a plant, or taking a shower, become aware of the cycle of water through the universe. Become aware of it travelling to where it is needed, for nourishment, growth or cleansing. Think of the water of baptism, by which you affirm your responsibility to the whole community. Think of water as embodying the possibility of rebirth, empowerment, and the hope of a renewed creation.

In the rainfall, in rivers and oceans, in watersheds, in your drinking and your washing, water cleanses, nourishes and heals.

Polluted water transforms nourishment into poison. Absence of water kills very quickly, but not quickly enough for the terrible suffering of thirsty people and land.

Become aware that within 10 years more than 40 per cent of the world's most vulnerable will suffer from water shortages.

For I will pour water on the thirsty land, and streams on
the dry ground.

Isaiah 44.3

earth and smell

When you are next in a garden, crumble some soil in your bare hands
and smell its rich aromas. Think of the life growing in the soil, the way
the soil nurtures and sustains new life, holds the seeds and shelters
the roots, becomes the foundation from which the plant grows. If you
are weeding, notice how the earth holds on to its own as you gently
dislodge roots from the soil. Notice how the actions of your hands
affect the soil well or badly. Become aware of the cycle of life and
death; crucifixion and resurrection:

> 'Very truly, I tell you, unless a grain of wheat falls into the
> earth and dies, it remains just a single grain; but if it dies,
> it bears much fruit.'

John 12.24

environmental organizations, contacts and web sites

There is an enormous amount of positive activity for the environment within the Church and between it and other partners. Nearly every diocese of the Church of England has a Diocesan Environment Officer, who may be the first port of call to becoming more involved. Their contact details can be obtained from the Church of England web site (www.cofe.anglican.org). There are web sites where information can be obtained about individual ecological footprints (the amount of resources a person consumes to sustain his/her lifestyle) and those of organizations or churches. Other web sites are helpful for improving consumption records. A list of these web sites is given below, together with the web sites of other environmental organizations. Their inclusion here does not constitute endorsement. First, however, there is a short description of the main national environmental organizations with which the Church has worked over the years.

The Alliance of Religions and Conservation (ARC)

Founded in 1995, ARC works with eleven of the world's faiths on environmental and development projects. Its work with the Anglican Church currently involves three major projects. The first is with the Manchester Diocese, where an ARC consultant is examining the management of the diocese's resources in relation to its recently adopted environmental policy. Resources include the diocese's churchyards, energy use, schools and building stock. The second project is called *3iG*, an Interfaith, International Investment Group, which faiths can join with a view to jointly and severally investing their funds positively in the light of their teachings and outlook. The third project is the Cistercian Way Project in Wales, which will create a long-distance pilgrimage route and initiate local sustainability projects along the way. This project will reach some of the most economically depressed communities in Wales.

contact

Alliance of Religions and Conservation
3 Wynnstay Grove, Fallowfield, Manchester M14 6XG
Tel. 0161 248 5731
Fax 0161 248 5736
jeannied@arcworld.org
www.arcworld.org

Anglican Communion Environmental Network (ACEN)

ACEN was created in response to a request by the Lambeth Conference of 1998 and became an official network of the Anglican Communion in 2002, following a successful Congress in South Africa held before the UN World Summit on Sustainable Development. It seeks to promote communication between Christians from every part of the Anglican Communion who are engaged in practical action and advocacy for the stewardship of creation.

contact

Revd Canon Dr Eric Beresford
Anglican Communion Office, St Andrew's House, 16 Tavistock Crescent, London W11 1AP
Tel. 020 7313 3900
Fax: 020 7313 3999
Eric.beresford@anglicancommunion.org
www.aco.org/ethics_technology

A Rocha UK

Launched in early 2001, A Rocha UK is a Christian conservation organization that works with individuals and organizations of many beliefs and backgrounds. Their main project focus is A Rocha Living Waterways, creating 'a greener, cleaner Southall and Hayes' in heavily built-up, multi-racial West London. This includes educational programmes for all ages in the Minet Country Park, a restored 36.4 hectare wasteland site between Southall and Hayes. A Rocha Living Waterways aims to be a catalyst in helping local communities understand, respect and enjoy the local environment. A Rocha has been welcomed by the faith communities in Southall: the common agenda of 'creation care' is seen as an opportunity for building on shared values. A community environmental centre accommodates A Rocha's UK offices and up to eight visitors, providing a focus for local work and enabling local people to come and find out about creation care and sustainable living.

contact

Revd David Bookless
A Rocha UK Director
1 Lancaster Road, Southall, Middlesex UB1 1NP
Dave.Bookless@arocha.org
www.arocha.org

The Arthur Rank Centre

The Arthur Rank Centre is an independent institution working on a number of initiatives relating to rural affairs. Dr Jill Hopkinson, who is based at the Arthur Rank Centre, is the Rural Affairs Officer for the Church of England. There are a number of activities run by the Centre that relate to the environment, including Eco-Congregation (see below), and the Living Churchyard project which now has some 6,000 burial grounds in approved environmental management. The Arthur Rank Centre works closely with national bodies in all aspects of rural affairs. Its work with farmers and rural communities, related to policy, economics, ethics, environment and pastoral care, has been highly commended. It has produced useful worship material for Harvest Festival and Rogationtide.

contact

Dr Jill Hopkinson, Church of England National Rural Officer, and
Revd Dr Gordon Gatward OBE, Director
The Arthur Rank Centre
National Agricultural Centre, Stoneleigh Park, Warwickshire CV8 2LZ
Tel. 024 7685 3060
Fax 024 7641 4808
info@arthurrankcentre.org.uk
www.arthurrankcentre.org.uk

Christian Ecology Link

Formed in 1981, Christian Ecology Link (CEL) is an ecumenical organization committed to taking care of God's creation. Its primary aim is to encourage Christians to integrate awareness of their environmental impact into their faith and lifestyle. CEL publishes a magazine (*Green Christian*), a news-sheet for display in churches (*ChurchLink*), and a comprehensive web site that is updated weekly. CEL is currently focusing on two campaigns, one on climate change entitled *Operation Noah*, which encourages individuals to switch to green energy and join the campaign for Contraction and Convergence, and one on food promoting the *LOAF* principles: Locally produced, Organically grown, Animal friendly and Fairly traded. CEL holds an annual conference as well as other events for its members.

contact

Laura Deacon, Information Officer
CEL, 3 Bond Street, Lancaster LA1 3ER
Tel. 01524 33858
Info@ christian-ecology.org.uk
www.christian-ecology.org.uk

The Conservation Foundation

The Conservation Foundation was launched in 1982 to help build bridges between industry, commerce, academia and the environment. It has done this through award schemes, educational projects, conferences, seminars, publications, radio and television programmes. It has worked in partnership with the Church of England on a number of projects, including Yews for the Millennium, the Parish Pump network, and a series of awareness-raising workshops funded by DEFRA held in each diocese. The Foundation provides a regular newsletter to its Parish Pumps with essential information for enthusiastic environmentalists.

contact

David Shreeve, Director
The Conservation Foundation, 1 Kensington Gore, London SW7 0AR
Tel. 020 7591 3111
Fax 020 7591 3110
info@conservationfoundation.co.uk
www.conservationfoundation.co.uk

CTBI Environmental Issues Network

The Environmental Issues Network (EIN) was established in 1990 to provide a forum for representatives drawn from those churches who are members of what is now Churches Together in Britain and Ireland (CTBI) and other Christian organizations, to consider local, national and global environmental and ecological issues. Its objectives are to act as a network to exchange news and information to enrich mutual work, promote ecumenical cooperation and avoid wasteful duplication.

EIN considers, reflects and comments on specific environmental issues and responds to requests from both church and secular bodies.

contact

Professor R. J. (Sam) Berry, Chair of EIN,
Quarfseter, 4 Sackville Close, Sevenoaks, Kent TN13 3QD
Tel. 01732 451907
Fax 01732 464253

Eco-Congregation

Eco-Congregation is an environmental resource for churches throughout Britain and Ireland and is available to all Christian denominations. Eco-Congregation material enables local churches to understand environmental issues within the context of their Christian faith, and to take practical action. A simple environmental audit – the 'Church Check-Up' – is provided to help congregations assess what they are already doing and determine future priorities. They can then access a range of resource modules, including theology and worship materials for young and old, assistance in improving energy use in the church building, and managing finances. Eco-Congregation is delivered in England from the Arthur Rank Centre, and in Scotland by a partnership between the Society, Religion and Technology Project (SRT) of the Church of Scotland and the environmental charity Keep Scotland Beautiful (KSB).

contact

Jo Rathbone
Eco-Congregation Coordinator (England and Wales)
The Arthur Rank Centre, Stoneleigh Park, Warwickshire CV8 2LZ
Tel. 024 7685 3061
ecocongregation@rase.org.uk
www.ecocongregation.org

Victoria Beale
Eco-Congregation Coordinator (Scotland)
Assistant Director of the Society, Religion and Technology Project
John Knox House, 45 High Street, Edinburgh EH1 1SR
Tel. 0131 556 2953
srtp@srtp.org.uk
www.ecocongregation.org/scotland

The Environmental Working Group of the National Church Institutions (NCIs)

Convened in 1999, this group represents the Church Commissioners, Archbishops' Council, Lambeth Palace, the Corporation of Church House and the Pensions Board. It aims to raise awareness of the impact on the environment of the NCIs' working practices. It has generated an overarching environmental policy for the NCIs, a purchasing policy and separate departmental environmental policies.

contact

Jo Winn-Smith
Church Commissioners, 1 Millbank, London SW1P 3JZ
Tel. 020 7898 1661
Jo.winn-smith@c-of-e.org.uk
www.cofe.anglican.org

The European Christian Environmental Network (ECEN)

ECEN enables the churches of Europe and Christian groups involved in environmental work to share information, pool common experiences and encourage each other in being a united witness to caring for God's creation. ECEN was set up on 24 October 1998 at a meeting of environmental representatives from 26 countries at Vilemov in the Czech Republic. The network embraces a wide variety of church traditions and an equally broad range of environmental work. This includes policy issues (such as climate change, transport, water, genetic engineering), practical action (including eco-management of church premises) and promoting an awareness of God's creation in worship and liturgy.

contact

Victoria Beale (details as above)
www.ecen.org

The John Ray Initiative (JRI)

JRI is an educational charity which brings together scientific and Christian understandings of the environment to promote the twin themes of sustainable development and environmental stewardship. It is named after the Essex-born naturalist and theologian John Ray (1627–1705). It was set up in 1997 by a group of scientists and is a registered charity. JRI believes in a strong and open scientific base to counter misunderstanding and prejudice, because God has set us in a world where we need to understand what is there, where the discoveries of science (within their limits) are as much a part of God's world as the revealed word of God. JRI has responded to a hunger among Christian believers to integrate their concern for the environment with their faith, or their scientific profession with their beliefs, and provides modules for distance learning courses. It is also developing a 'learning community' which could become a network of thinking Christian environmentalists.

contact

David Thistlethwaite
The John Ray Initiative, University of Gloucestershire QW 212, Francis Close Hall, Swindon Road, Cheltenham GL50 4AZ
Tel. 01242 543 580
Fax 087 0132 3943
jri@glos.ac.uk
www.jri.org.uk

Operation EDEN

Operation EDEN is based in the Church of England Diocese of Liverpool. It aims to make a key contribution to local environmental action, economic development and sustainability. It is a pilot initiative to enable locally based faith agencies to be involved in transforming the environment, and it is hoped that this can be adapted for use in other areas. The project is based on a partnership engaging a network of community volunteers forging links with all faith communities. EDEN will distribute a £160k fund to support small environmental improvement projects, including the development of social enterprises, biodiversity, the efficient use of resources and remediation of brown-field sites.

contact

Annie Merry, Tom Veitch or Sr Marjorie Griffin
Church House, 1 Hanover Street, Liverpool L1 3DW
tel. 0151 7052130
www.operation-eden.org.uk

The Religious Education and Environment Project

REEP, the Religious Education and Environment Project, was set up by the charity Friends of the Centre in 1994 to encourage the study of environmental issues in the context of religious insights. It was born of a conviction that at the centre of the world's great religious traditions is a system of ideas and a corresponding set of values and practices which can provide people with effective tools for reflecting on, and responding to, the crises that face our planet. REEP believes that Religious Education in schools – and indeed theology in higher education establishments and education in theological colleges – should include those elements of religious teaching which emphasize human responsibility towards the natural world. Its work is disseminated only through its web site.

contact

www.reep.org

Religion, Science and the Environment Symposia

This movement was originally conceived in 1988 on the Isle of Patmos, at a meeting of environmental and religious leaders. It was established out of concern for the water environment of the planet, which covers seven-tenths of the earth's surface. This concern is both theological and scientific, and one of the underlying purposes of the movement is to establish common ground on the implications and imperatives of this ecological crisis between representatives of faith communities, professional scientists and environmental NGOs. The leading spirit of 'Religion, Science and the Environment' is His All Holiness Bartholomew, Ecumenical Patriarch of the Christian Orthodox Church of Constantinople. The movement operates through Symposium study voyages, each of which has several hundred participants. Their aim is to debate the plight of the world's waters; to visit sites of special concern; to meet officials and NGO representatives in the countries visited; to propose solutions; and to initiate schemes or institutions for environmental cooperation and education.

contact

Ms Maria Becket, Symposium Coordinator
Walton House, Walton Street, London SW3 2JH
Tel. 020 7589 1094
Fax 020 7589 2650
rsecommittee@rsesymposia.org
www.rsesymposia.org

The Society, Religion and Technology Project (SRT), Church of Scotland

The SRT Project was set up in 1970 by the Church of Scotland to examine ethical questions about current and future technologies. Since 1992 its main policy focus has been on bioethics, sustainable development, energy/climate change, and science and society. SRT engages directly with those in research, industry, policy and regulation, and is involved with several national and international advisory bodies.

contact

Dr Donald Bruce
Director, Society, Religion and Technology Project
Church of Scotland, John Knox House, 45 High Street, Edinburgh EH1 1SR
Tel. 0131 556 2953
Fax 0131 556 7478
srtp@srtp.org.uk
www.srtp.org.uk

contacts within the Church of England

There are Diocesan Environment Officers in most Church of England dioceses. There is also a Bishops' Environmental Group, with individual episcopal spokespersons for different aspects of the environment. Names and contact details can be obtained from national policy adviser on environmental issues at Church House in Westminster (020 7898 1523; Claire.foster@c-of-e.org.uk).

web sites

other organizations

Carbon Trust www.carbontrust.co.uk (for information on living a low-carbon life)

Christian Aid www.christian-aid.org.uk

Energy Saving Trust www.est.org.uk (set up by the Government after the Earth Summit in Rio de Janeiro, 1992, to address energy issues)

Friends of the Earth www.foe.org

Global Commons Institute www.gci.org.uk (focuses on Contraction and Convergence)

Greenpeace www.greenpeace.org

Linking Environment and Farming www.leafuk.org

Tearfund www.tearfund.org

Trade Justice Movement www.tradejusticemovement.org.uk (signed up to by the Church of England)

The Vegetarian Society www.vegsoc.org (this web site has fascinating information about human consumption practices and their relative costs to the environment)

Wateraid www.wateraid.org.uk

World Wide Fund for Nature www.wwf.org

web sites for practical action

www.earthsummit.org from the UN summit on Sustainable Development, this web site has a wealth of material on every aspect

www.CO2.org calculates your CO^2 emissions

www.myfootprint.org calculates your ecological footprint

www.recycle-more.com information and competitions for recycling projects

www.getethical.com a directory of ecologically focused retailers

www.naturalcollection.com eco-friendly (and stylish) natural products for your home

www.bigbarn.co.uk tells you where you can buy local food in your postcode area

www.abel-cole.co.uk organic fruit and vegetables delivered

www.greenbabyco.com eco-friendly parenting

www.ltl.org.uk guidance for parents and teachers on safer and more sustainable transport for children

www.treeforall.org.uk Woodland Trust scheme to give every child in the country the chance to plant a tree

www.greenmetropolis.com secondhand bookshop

www.ecotricity.co.uk wind turbine energy source

www.transportenergy.org.uk grants for using greener cars

www.searchnbn.net 15 million observations of wildlife organized by the National Biodiversity Network Trust

www.woodsunderthreat.info the Woodland Trust gives the location of ancient woodlands and those under threat

www.activecitizenship.co.uk how to take an active role in your local community

www.defra.gov.uk/environment/pubaccess find out public information on air, water, land, flora and fauna, habitats, food, the built environment and health

www.rcep.org.uk Royal Commission on Environmental Pollution web site

www.energysavingtrust.co.uk advice and support for moving to greener energy sources

www.wen.org.uk Women's Environmental Network

notes

part one

1. John Robert McNeill, *Something New under the Sun: an environmental history of the twentieth-century world*, W. W. Norton & Company, 2000, p. 59.

2. John D. Zizioulas, 'Preserving God's Creation I: three lectures on theology and ecology', *King's Theological Review* XII:1, Spring 1989a, p. 4.

3. McNeill, *Something New under the Sun*, p. 3.

4. John Houghton, *Global Warming: the complete briefing*, Cambridge University Press, 1997, p. 13. The information in this section on the atmosphere is taken from Houghton, *Global Warming*; Thomas Graedel and Paul Crutzen, 'The changing atmosphere', in *Scientific American* 261:3, 1989, pp. 58–68; David Salstein, 'Mean properties of the atmosphere', in H. B. Singh (ed.), *Composition, Chemistry and Climate of the Atmosphere*, Van Nostrand Reinhold, 1995, pp. 19–49.

5. McNeill, *Something New under the Sun*, p. 103.

6. R. P. Turco, *Earth under Siege: from air pollution to global change*, Oxford University Press, 1997, p. 4.

7. McNeill, *Something New under the Sun*, p. 109.

8. T. S. Ledley, E. R. Sundquist, S. E. Schwartz, D. K. Hall, J. D. Fellows and T. L. Killeen, 'Climate change and greenhouse gases', American Geophysical Union, *EOS* 80:39, 28 September 1999.

9. Bill McGuire, *Climate Change 2004*, Benfield Hazard Research Centre, 2004, p. 1.

10. McGuire, *Climate Change 2004*, p, 1.

11. McNeill, *Something New under the Sun*, p. 111.

12. McNeill, *Something New under the Sun*, p. 119.

13. McNeill, *Something New under the Sun*, p. 135.

14. J. Timmons Roberts and Bradley C. Parks, *People and the Environment on the Edge: environmental vulnerability in Latin America and the Caribbean*, CIIR, 2004.

15. J. Thulin and A. Andrushaitis, 'The Baltic Sea under threat', a talk given to the Fifth Religion, Science and Environment Symposium of the Ecumenical Patriarch, 2 June 2003.

16. Quoted in McNeill, *Something New under the Sun*, p. 149.

17. Earthscan, *Global Environment Outlook 3*, United Nations Environment Programme, 2002, p. 305.

18. F. Pearce, 'The world water crisis', *New Scientist*, 28 August 2004, p. 6.

19. McNeill, *Something New under the Sun*, p. 190.

20. R. W. Arnold, I. Szaboles and V. O. Targulian, *Global Soil Change*, International Institute for Applied Systems Analysis, 1990, p. 77.

21. Roger L. Hooke, 'On the efficacy of humans and geomorphic agents', Geological Society of America, *GSA Today* 4, p. 217.

22. E. O. Wilson, *The Diversity of Life*, Penguin Books, 2001, p. 332.

23. Wilson, *The Diversity of Life*, p. 335

part two

1. Lambeth, *Transformation and Renewal: the official report of the Lambeth Conference*, Morehouse Publishing, 1998, pp. 86–92.

2. E. O. Wilson, *The Diversity of Life*, p. 12.

3. For example, H. Eaton, 'Response to Rosemary Radford Ruether: ecofeminism and theology – challenges, confrontations and reconstructions', in Dieter T. Hessel and Rosemary Radford Ruether (eds), *Christianity and Ecology*, Harvard University Press, 2000, p. 115.

4. O. Clement, *On Human Being: a spiritual anthropology*, trans. J. Hummerstone, New City, 2000, p. 136.

5. Evelyn Underhill, *Practical Mysticism*, General Publishing Co. Ltd, 2000, pp. 48–9.

6. Jürgen Moltmann, *God in Creation: The Gifford Lectures*, SCM Press, 1985, p. 31.

7. Isaiah 65; and S. McFague, 'An ecological Christology: does Christianity have it?', in Dieter T. Hessel and Rosemary Radford Ruether, *Christianity and Ecology*, Harvard University Press, 2000, p. 32.

8. Julian of Norwich *Revelations of Divine Love*, trans. James Walsh SJ, Anthony Clarke Books, 1973, pp. 67–8.

9. Jacques Lusseyran, *And there was light*, trans. E. R. Cameron, Parabola Books, 1994, p. 27.

10. Anne Primavesi, *Sacred Gaia: holistic theology and earth system science*, Routledge, 2000, p. 12.

11. Eaton, 'Response to Rosemary Radford Ruether', p. 120.

12. Wilson, *The Diversity of Life*, p. 328.

13. Fr John Chryssavgis (ed.), *Cosmic Grace: Humble Prayer: the ecological vision of the Green Patriarch Bartholomew I*, Wm B. Eerdmans Publishing Co., 2003, p. 91.

14. Chryssavgis, *Cosmic Grace*, p. 23.

15. Aidan Hart, 'The pain of the earth: a cry for change', a talk given to the European Christian Environmental Network, Minsk, Belarus, 29 May 2001, p. 3.

16. Hart, 'The pain of the earth: a cry for change', p. 3.

17. Simone Weil, *Waiting for God*, Perennial Classics, 2001, p. 62.

18. Chryssavgis, *Cosmic Grace*, p. 33.

19. Fyodor Dostoevsky, *The Karamazov Brothers*, trans. Ignat Avsey, Oxford University Press, 1994, pp. 399–400.

20. John D. Zizioulas, 'Preserving God's Creation III: three lectures on theology and ecology', *King's Theological Review XIII:1*, Spring, 1990, p. 4.

21. Hart, 'The pain of the earth: a cry for change', p. 7.

22. Wendell Berry, *The Gift of Good Land*, North Point Press, 1981, p. 21.

23. J. Jones, *Jesus and the Earth*, SPCK, 2003 p. 14

24. Irenaeus, *Against Heresies*, 5.33.

25. Moltmann, *God in Creation*, p. 188.

26. R. S. Thomas, 'The Bright Field' in *Laboratories of the Spirit*, London, Macmillan, 1975, reproduced by permission.

27. D. H. Lawrence, 'Shadows'.

28. Lambeth, *Transformation and Renewal*, p. 92.

29. John V. Taylor, *Enough is Enough*, SCM Press, 1975, p. 52.

30. Taylor, *Enough is Enough*, p. 50.

31. Jones, *Jesus and the Earth*, p. 59.

part three

1. David Fiske, 'Sustainable Development: presentation at Wakefield Parish Pump Workshop', *Parish Pump Newsletter* 10, 2004.

2. C. Borgstrom Hansson, 'Treading lightly: understanding and reducing the human footprint', in *Symposium V The Baltic Sea: a common heritage, a shared responsibility*, 2003, p. 2; see web site www.rsesymposia.org

3. J. Jones, *Jesus and the Earth*, p. 42.

4. Rowan Williams, 'Changing the myths we live by', lecture delivered at Lambeth Palace, 5 July 2004, p. 7.

5. John V. Taylor, *Enough is Enough*, p. 79.

recommended reading

Ian Barbour, *Nature, Human Nature and God*, SPCK, 2002.

Margaret Barker, *Temple Theology*, SPCK, 2003.

R. J. Berry, *God's Book of Works: The Gifford Lectures*, T&T Clark, 2003.

O. Clement, *On Human Being: a spiritual anthropology*, trans. J. Hummerstone, New City, 2000.

Fr John Chryssavgis (ed.) *Cosmic Grace: Humble Prayer: the ecological vision of the Green Patriarch Bartholomew 1*, Wm B. Eerdmans Publishing Co., 2003.

T. Cooper, *Sustaining the Earth*, St John's College, 2000.

C. Deane-Drummond, *The Ethics of Nature*, Blackwell, 2004.

Earthscan, *Global Environment Outlook 3*, United Nations Environment Programme, 2002.

E. Echlin, *The Cosmic Circle: Jesus and ecology*, Columba Press, 2004.

Jeffery M. Golliher, 'This fragile earth our island home: the environmental crisis', in Ian T. Douglas and Piu-Lan Kwok (eds), *Beyond Colonial Anglicanism: the Anglican Church in the 21st century*, Church Publishing Inc., 2001.

David Gosling, *Religion and Ecology in India and southeast Asia*, Routledge, 2001.

J. Hart, *Environmental Theology*, Paulist Press, 2004.

Dieter T. Hessel and Rosemary Radford Ruether, *Christianity and Ecology*, Harvard University Press, 2000.

John Houghton, *Global Warming: the complete briefing*, Cambridge University Press, 1997.

J. Jones, *Jesus and the Earth*, SPCK, 2003.

Bjorn Lomberg, *The Skeptical Environmentalist*, Cambridge University Press, 2001.

M. Low, *Cherish the Earth: reflections on a living planet*, Wild Goose Publications, 2003.

Jacques Lusseyran, *And there was light*, trans. E. R. Cameron, Parabola Books, 1994.

Alistair McGrath, *The Re-enchantment of Nature*, Hodder & Stoughton, 2002.

J. R. McNeill, *Something New under the Sun: an environmental history of the twentieth-century world*, W. W. Norton & Company, 2000.

Aubrey Meyer, *Contraction and Convergence: the global solution to climate change*, Green Books Ltd, 2000.

Max Oeschlaeger, *Caring for Creation*, Yale University Press, 1994.

M. Palmer and V. Finlay, *Faith in Conservation: new approaches to religions and the environment*, World Bank, 2003.

G. Prance, *The Earth under Threat,* Wild Goose Publications, 1996.

Anne Primavesi, *Sacred Gaia: holistic theology and earth system science*, Routledge, 2000.

Religion, Science and Environment, Reports of each of the Symposia hosted by HAH Ecumenical Patriarch Bartholomew I, 1997–2003. See www.rsesymposia.org

E. F. Schumacher, *Small is Beautiful*, Sphere Books Ltd, 1974.

W. J. Short DFM, *Poverty and Joy*, Darton, Longman & Todd, 1999.

John V. Taylor, *Enough is Enough*, SCM Press, 1975.

D. Wilkinson, *The Message of Creation: encountering the Lord of the universe*, Inter-Varsity Press, 2002.

E. O. Wilson, *The Diversity of Life*, Penguin Books, 2001.

Evelyn Underhill, *Practical Mysticism*, General Publishing Co. Ltd, 2000.

Simone Weil, *Waiting for God*, Perennial Classics, 2001.

World Council of Churches, Justice, Peace and Creation, *Solidarity with Victims of Climate Change*, World Council of Churches, 2002.